TRUDEAU

TRUDEAU

IMAGES OF CANADA'S PASSIONATE STATESMAN

Introduction and Interviews by HELEN BRANSWELL

Edited by PATTI TASKO

THE CANADIAN PRESS

John Wiley & Sons Canada, Ltd.

Library and Archives Canada Cataloguing in Publication

Trudeau : images of Canada's passionate statesman / The Canadian Press ; Patti Tasko, editor.

ISBN 978-0-470-67967-8

1. Trudeau, Pierre Elliott, 1919-2000—Pictorial works.
2. Canada—Politics and government—20th century—Pictorial works. 3. Liberal Party of Canada—History—20th century—Pictorial works. 4. Prime ministers—Canada—Pictorial works.
I. Tasko, Patti II. Canadian Press

FC626.T7T778 2010   971.064'4092   C2010-901919-9

PRODUCTION CREDITS
Cover and interior design: Diana Sullada
Printer: Friesens

Front jacket photo: Gail Harvey
Inside Front jacket: Doug Ball
Back jacket: Top and middle: Peter Bregg; Bottom: Doug Ball

John Wiley & Sons Canada, Ltd.
6045 Freemont Blvd.
Mississauga, Ontario L5R 4J3

Printed in Canada

1 2 3 4 5 FP 14 13 12 11 10

ENVIRONMENTAL BENEFITS STATEMENT

John Wiley & Sons - Canada saved the following resources by printing the pages of this book on chlorine free paper made with 10% post-consumer waste.

TREES	WATER	SOLID WASTE	GREENHOUSE GASES
11 FULLY GROWN	5,138 GALLONS	312 POUNDS	1,067 POUNDS

 Calculations based on research by Environmental Defense and the Paper Task Force. Manufactured at Friesens Corporation

(Previous) Trudeau, carrying his son Justin, at a Government House garden party. Ottawa, August 1973. Rod MacIvor

" … what was predictable was that he was unpredictable."

Trudeau at the Chateau Laurier hotel
during Liberal leadership convention.
Ottawa, 1968. Ted Grant

"Just watch me."

Was ever an instruction less needed? Was ever an invitation so heeded?

We could not take our eyes off Pierre Elliot Trudeau. The man mesmerized us. Love him, hate him—and both emotions applied, in varying measures at varying times—Canadians could not help but gaze with wonder at the enigmatic character who led the country, with but a brief interruption, from 1968 to 1984.

Prime ministers had been sombre, staid gentlemen in dark suits. Along came Trudeau. Politics became Technicoloured.

It's right there in one of the first shots of Trudeau as prime minister. He and key members of his government—John Turner, Jean Marchand, Gérard Pelletier—are striding across the lawn of Rideau Hall on their way to the swearing in of his first cabinet. There's a swagger. There's attitude. There are Ray-Bans.

"It makes politics seem cool," Trudeau's son, Alexandre, says many years later, a note of wonder in his voice.

Alexandre and Justin Trudeau, the late prime minister's surviving sons, sat down in 2002 and reviewed the photographs in this book. The interview took place in the formal living room of the elegant Montreal home where they lived following their father's retirement from politics. Atop a piano in that room sat a framed copy of one of the photographs this book contains—a shot of Trudeau and his three sons acknowledging the applause and cheers following his 1984 farewell speech to the Liberal Party.

His sons, handsome, eloquent, composed young men, laughed and reminisced about the man we knew as the dominant Canadian politician of the last half of the 20TH century, the man they knew as their devoted dad. They shared observations and motivations, recounting Trudeau's explanations of the history he had a hand in making and descriptions of world figures with whom he met.

Mostly they shared memories. Their words tumbled over one another as they recalled three small children piling into Trudeau's Mercedes convertible for the drive to the prime minister's country retreat at Harrington Lake in the Gatineau hills north of Ottawa. Or travelling the globe with their father. Or learning to test their limits by jumping from trees, walls, statues.

Their insights give us a glimpse of the man behind the photographs, a man we but rarely saw.

Occasionally, though, the camera caught the private man. You can see it in a photograph of Trudeau dancing nose-to-nose with his beautiful young wife, Margaret. Trudeau was the consummate showman, but that intimate image isn't about show.

"My father was searching for my mother his entire life. And he found her. And he loved her with everything he had and everything that he could. And she loved him absolutely right back … that picture of them dancing is all about that perfect love," Justin says.

Equally unguarded are the haunting images of Trudeau and his family after the funeral of his youngest son, Michel, who died in an avalanche in 1998. Alexandre and Justin look stricken. Margaret Trudeau can barely stand. Trudeau looks like a man destroyed.

"I think you can just see it, the way he's looking at us. He looks very empty," says Ryan Remiorz, the Canadian Press photographer who took those photos.

Unguarded moments were rare, however. Wherever Trudeau went, the cameras went too. And when cameras were around, Trudeau knew it was time to perform, his sons say.

"Acting all the time," Alexandre insists.

Did he act in private as well? The question makes the brothers laugh.

"No," Alexandre retorts. "Never," Justin adds.

Take the famous shrug, an image former Canadian Press photographer Peter Bregg froze during a 1981 news conference on the patriation of the Constitution. Without knowing the subject matter under discussion, Trudeau's sons know exactly what that gesture was meant to say—but insist it was a face their father never showed at home.

"We never saw that face. That's `What do you want me to do here? What do you expect of me?' But he would never say that to us because, you know, he knew exactly what we expected of him and he lived up to it," Justin says.

"He was a very different guy in front of the camera than from behind," Alexandre continues. "He was kind of a shy guy … a quiet, shy person. So when the cameras went on, he sort of caricatured himself.

"You're never just who you are, when you're in the public view. You create a persona."

And what a complex persona he forged. A towering intellect, one political opponents underestimated at their peril. A man who was not classically handsome—slight in stature, retreating hair line, with a hawkish nose and prominent teeth—yet so charismatic women fell under his spell as if he were a film star. A serious man, yet a man whose actions were often anything but. Perhaps most curiously, a man who indulged his insouciant sense of whimsy at precisely the time when most political figures would have been intent on being their most statesmanlike: when framed within the lens of a news photographer's camera.

Most public figures are desperate to ensure they are not captured on film appearing frivolous or silly. They—or their aides—go to great lengths to ensure unflattering angles or behaviours are not exposed.

If there's a politicians' handbook it probably says: *When in public, look thoughtful and engaged. Don't grimace or yawn. No fingers near the nose. Don't display boredom and annoyance. Don't make childish faces. Above all, don't don strange headwear.* All it takes is one fleeting moment in a goofy hat, a hair net, a helmet donned backwards. An undignified image is frozen in time, often to haunt the hapless subject for years to come.

A good photographer needs only a second to create years of regret.

"I've been on many trips where prime ministers, queens and emperors receive something. You hand it to somebody because you're going to look like Gilles Duceppe … or Jean Chrétien, with the helmet on backwards," says Bregg.

Bregg is referring to a 1997 picture of the Bloc Québécois leader in a hair net during an election tour of a cheese factory and Chrétien who donned a military helmet back-to-front during a visit to Canadian troops in Bosnia.

Trudeau broke all the rules, including the headgear taboo. He posed for photographers in a fur hat with a wolverine head perched on top. The wolverine's face, wide across the cheekbones, narrowing to the snout, actually mirrors Trudeau's own. What other political leader would have dared worn that hat?

"He always pulled it off," Remiorz says. "And he made it seem—and I'm not saying it wasn't—but it always came across as very sincere. His lighter side. A guy that liked to have fun. A guy that liked to fool around. To be active.

"It was very difficult to take a bad picture of him."

Perhaps it was the fact Trudeau didn't mind mocking himself. Or that he had the confidence to know he could pull it off. How else can one explain a prime minister who allowed himself to be photographed dancing, in his own flowing blue silk jallabiya, with a Saudi sheik? Strangling himself with a tie? Sticking his tongue out at a photographer? Or wearing a flowing cape and foppish fedora to a Grey Cup game? "It's over the top, even for him," Justin says with an incredulous shake of his head.

"He understood the power of a single image," Remiorz says. "He used us. We used him. And it was a very nice working relationship. As long as we didn't pry, he tolerated us quite well, I think."

"He was the master, absolute master, of the photo op. The non-photo op," agrees former Canadian Press photographer Doug Ball. "He liked the shock effect. And he liked to be different."

Ball is the lightening-fingered lensman who captured what may be the single most famous image of Trudeau: the infamous Buckingham Palace pirouette, behind the back of the departing Queen.

Why did Trudeau do it? Was it an expression of disdain for the Queen? His sons say no. He told them he was poking a bit of fun at the situation, where leaders of the Group of Seven countries had just been jockeying for spots closest to the Queen for a photo opportunity. That wasn't Trudeau's thing. He was off at the end of the line. After the photo, the Queen and the politicians began to walk off. The photographers were being ushered from the room. Trudeau succumbed to one of his fits of whimsy.

"It wasn't disrespectful," Alexandre insists. "It was playful."

"He's just defusing a bit the situation, as much for himself as for anyone else."

Ball says Trudeau told him later he had thought all the photographers had moved out of range when he performed his little twirl, a move that became a signature piece, 'punctuation,' as his sons put it, for special occasions.

Did Trudeau really think no one would notice? "I think he just did it for the hell of it," Ball says. "But he knew—not that he spent a long time thinking about it—but if it got captured or anything like that, that wouldn't be bad either."

In fact, Trudeau revelled in challenging photographers to catch him "goofing," as his sons describe his at-times outlandish antics. "Keep your eye on me," his actions seemed to say. "But you'd better be sharp. Better be quick."

"If you were around him, you knew—if you were travelling with him or at home or if you were covering him on the Hill—that almost every day you could almost bank on the fact that Trudeau was going to give you a picture of some kind that was going to be noteworthy and usable," recalls Chuck Mitchell, the Canadian Press photographer who caught Trudeau on film with Barbra Streisand.

"And if you were on your toes, you got it. And if you weren't, you went hungry that day."

That's because the mercurial Trudeau was a one-take kind of guy. He'd spin or grin or grimace or glare, all without a second's notice. If a photographer missed it—and many did, especially in the days before cameras came equipped with motor drives—he or she faced the unenviable task of explaining to the boss why the competition had the shot.

"I think there were times he would do things, not fearing the consequences," Bregg says. "Then you'd see a bunch of photographers dropping lenses, scrambling. 'Do it again! Do it again!' Never. It was rare that he ever did it again."

Nor was he interested in working with photographers on set-up shots. He might crack a whip or toss a Frisbee or sling a baby over his hip and give a lucky photographer an award-winning photo. But ask him to do it? Forget about it.

"That was the thing about him: If you had to plan something, he didn't want to be part of it," Bregg recalls.

"If it came by accident, he loved it. He didn't mind performing the part. But I know that the many times I would say: 'Would you like to do this for me?' he'd say 'No, no, you do what you have to do. I'll do what I want.' "

"I think he felt: Why have to force yourself to be that way… staid and dignified? Dignity doesn't come necessarily from standing stiff," Justin explains. "Dignity is doing your job intelligently, passionately. He wasn't a fan of rules of convention, in any direction," Alexandre adds. "Just because he's in a suit and has a high job doesn't mean he's not prepared to dash or run or jump. He was just enjoying life…. No job was going to stop him from doing that."

In the following pages, the photographs that are part of the legacy of the Trudeau years show us this man. Taken by some of the country's best photojournalists, these images from The Canadian Press archives remind us of the man who bewitched us and bewildered us, who engaged us and enraged us, a man who challenged us—like he did his sons—to test our limits. Enjoy.

— Helen Branswell
The Canadian Press

Trudeau waits for results of Liberal leadership race.
Ottawa, April 1968. Chuck Mitchell

ALEXANDRE: He was a very different guy in front of the cameras than from behind. He was kind
               of a shy guy. Quiet, shy person. So when the cameras went on, he'd sort of
               caricature himself …

JUSTIN: And go overboard.

ALEXANDRE: You're never just who you are, when you're in the public view. You create a persona.

CHUCK
MITCHELL: He never looked worried. It was just his nature. He was very good at covering
               his emotions.

JUSTIN: It's a classic picture—him and that smile.

ALEXANDRE: He was ready to take it on. (But) I think he was pretty surprised by all this turn of events (Trudeau was part of a committee to find a new leader and only ran himself after Jean Marchand refused.)

JUSTIN: He knew he could do it very well. But at the same time . . .

ALEXANDRE: . . . didn't want it to be powered by his own ambition.

JUSTIN: It was very important to him to do things to make a difference. That's why he chose to go to Ottawa, that's why he chose to do this stuff. But to actually do it by becoming prime minister?

ALEXANDRE: He found that sort of hard ambition—hard political ambition especially—loathsome.

JUSTIN: Distasteful. Because it's ambition for ambition's sake. He never lost sight of the things that he could do and he wanted to do. It was a means to an end. Never an end in itself, to become prime minister. It's a way of getting things done.

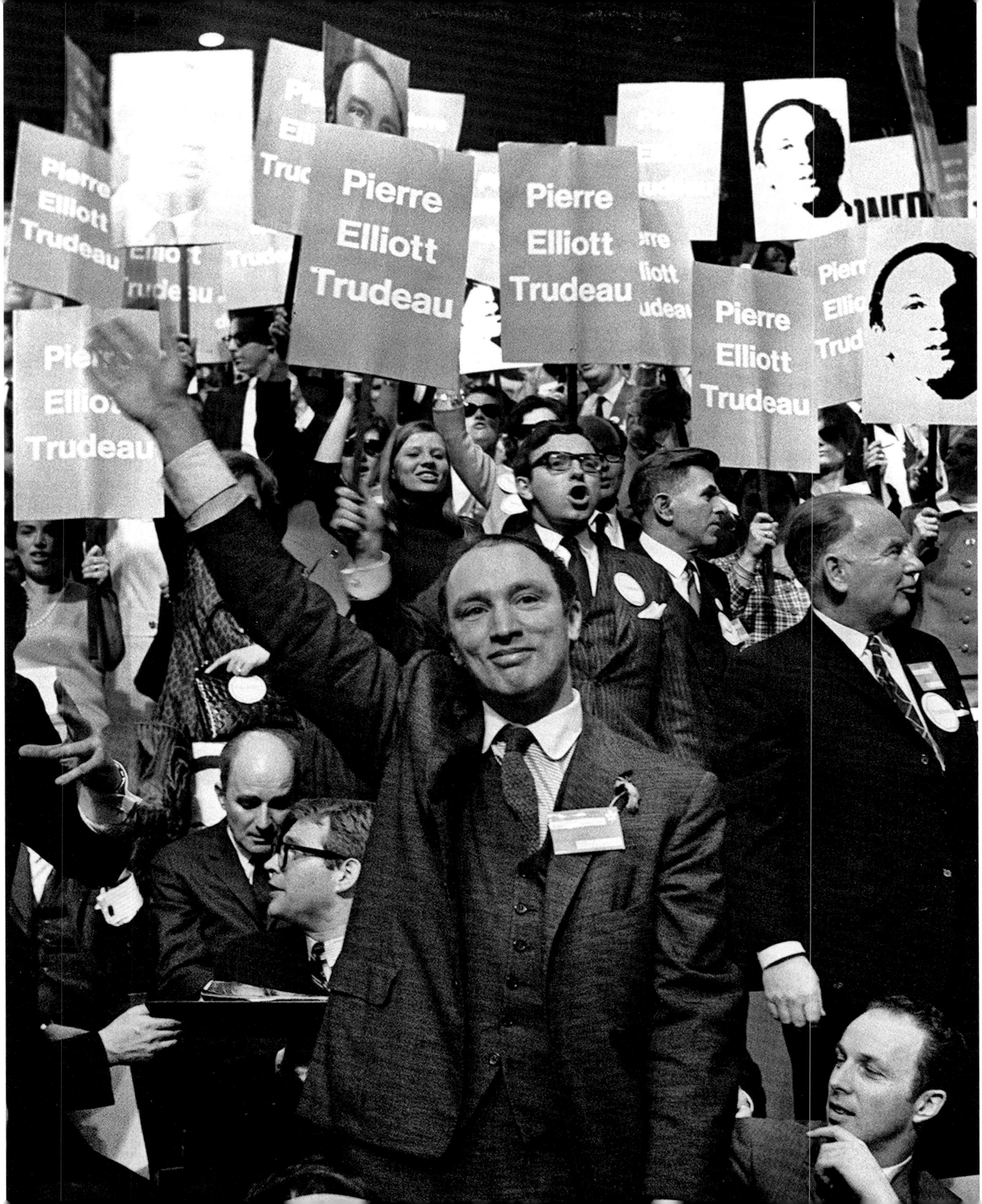

Trudeau outside Parliament Buildings.
Ottawa, April 1968. Peter Bregg

JUSTIN: He was an extremely active, fit person on his time off when he wasn't having to be prime minister. I think he felt: Why have to force yourself to be … staid and dignified? Dignity doesn't come necessarily from standing stiff.

ALEXANDRE: Dignity is doing your job intelligently, passionately. He wasn't a fan of rules of convention, in any direction.

PETER BREGG: These young girls all showed up and started bugging him for autographs. And in a split second, he just turned on a dime and ran. Because Trudeau was so new, his attitude was so new, what was predictable was that he was unpredictable.

Trudeau on the campaign trail.

Montreal, June 1968. Chuck Mitchell

ALEXANDRE: Jeez, that looks like a great party. I'd love to be there!

JUSTIN: Love to be there! Everyone watching while he's doing his thing.

ALEXANDRE: He was always a great prankster. And therefore: "OK, throw in the hat. But you'd better start dancing."

CHUCK
MITCHELL: You get off the bus and he does stuff like this. And bang! If you're not ready, you've missed it. Or if you decide you're going to walk over and grab some chips from the chip wagon over there, you'll see it from a distance. By the time you get back, you're in trouble. Somebody else has it.

Trudeau during a break in campaigning.
Oakville, Ontario, June 1968. Joe Horigan

ALEXANDRE: When he was in politics he used to swim every day in the evening … he was not an early riser…. Remember, we would go to school and he'd still be asleep? In Ottawa we'd go to school at eight.

JUSTIN: Oh, that's right. Just as we'd leave we'd go wake him up.

ALEXANDRE: And his aides used to say: "Don't try and get things done with him before two or something."

20

Showing his carnation to children at a housing project.
New Brunswick, 1969. Peter Bregg

Speaking to angry farmers.
Saskatoon, July 17, 1969. Peter Bregg

PETER BREGG: This is the famous confrontation where Trudeau said, "Why should I sell your wheat?" (The comment created the perception that Trudeau was dismissing the protestors' concerns as it was not widely reported that he had asked the question rhetorically and then answered it.)

CHUCK MITCHELL: All hell broke loose. Everything was flying. And they all started to get up and leave. Security wanted him out of there.... He shook them off and came back and sat down. And stood there, defiantly. He just said: 'No. You're not going to scare me away.'

Trudeau celebrates federal election win.

Montreal, June 1968. Chuck Mitchell

JUSTIN: He's got that, 'Oh, boy, here we go' (look). Incoming. Here it comes.

ALEXANDRE: '(It's) if I kiss you, I'm going to have to kiss 30 others. And they may not be all as pretty as you.'

Trudeau and members of his cabinet (James Richardson, D.C. Jamieson (partly hidden),
John Turner, Jean Marchand, Gérard Pelletier) arrive for swearing-in ceremony.
Ottawa, July 1968. DOUG BALL

JUSTIN: Quentin Tarantino stole this from us.

ALEXANDRE: It makes politicians seem cool, which I don't think they always seem these days.

ALEXANDRE: He really enjoyed the Inuit.

JUSTIN: He really loved the North.

ALEXANDRE: They just have such a powerful existence.

On Resolute Island.
Nunavut, July 1968. Peter Bregg

ALEXANDRE: I think another reason why he loved the North was because it was not sitting in meetings
… it was out on the land.

After being presented with honorary tie
at the National Press Club.
Ottawa, September 1968. Peter Bregg

JUSTIN: That reminds me of some of the stories and pictures he told us of his time in Paris and stuff.

ALEXANDRE: He was a legendary prankster with his friend Roger Lalonde…. They used to pull elaborate pranks, elaborate…. His old buddies were the ones he would joke with.

PETER BREGG: *(who says the picture was used worldwide, with the Paris newspaper Le Figaro saying how refreshing it was to see a politician doing this type of thing. Trudeau's staff didn't like it, however.)*
They called to voice their concern that we'd made Trudeau look awful in the world.
But hey, this is Trudeau. This was what was to come. Pirouettes and that kind of thing.

Trudeau with John Lennon and Yoko Ono, in his office.
Ottawa, December 1969. Peter Bregg

PETER BREGG: It was a photo op in the prime minister's office and that's where the media were setting up. I was downstairs at the front door (when Lennon and Ono arrived) and there was no one to meet them so I shook their hands and took them inside. Because all the cameras were already in the room, I couldn't stand up, so I got down on my knees before the prime minister. At one point, the prime minister said to them, "Look out for this guy" and they all looked down and I got the picture.

PETER BREGG: This was the first time we saw Margaret Trudeau, Margaret Sinclair. This was her coming out, I think, in public. They were skating around, so you know, Flash! Flash! Click! Click! So finally I called out: "Prime Minister, Prime Minister! Can we have the lady's name?" So . . . he says: "What do you think, Margaret? Should we tell them?" Margaret, OK! (*Bregg pantomimes jotting it down.*) So she says: "OK, Sinclair." So here's Margaret Sinclair.

Trudeau with Barbra Streisand at the National Arts Centre.

Ottawa, January 1970. Chuck Mitchell

ALEXANDRE: I'd always heard about this but I don't … I didn't even remember when this was.

JUSTIN: That's because it was before us, that's why … we have no memories of Barbra Streisand.

CHUCK
MITCHELL: That picture surprised everybody. In fact, I had to kind of pick myself up off the floor
to make the picture, when she stepped out of the car. I didn't even have a camera in my
hand when he arrived. I was just standing there watching. As she looked up, halfway out
of the car, I said: "Holy shit! It's Barbra Streisand!" After that, we always kept a sharp eye
to see if he was with somebody and whom he was with.

Trudeau on a dog sled.

Igloolik, Baffin Island, March 1970. Peter Bregg

PETER BREGG: It's not that I think he went looking for photo ops. But he appreciated that this was what we wanted.... That was the thing about him: If you had to plan something, he didn't want to be part of it. If it came by accident, he loved it. He didn't mind performing the part. But I know that the many times I would say: "Would you like to do this for me?" He'd say, "No, no, you do what you have to do, I'll do what I want."

Trudeau at Baker Lake.
Nunavut, March 1970. Peter Bregg

PETER BREGG: Somebody was standing by with a whip on this Arctic tour. And he just thought he'd try it out. So the guy gave him a quick lesson. "Here's how you do it." Crack! He did it. He was good. Everything he tried, he was good at. It's not an easy thing to do to flip a whip and have it snap at the end.

Trudeau arrives in Ottawa after tour of Northern Canada.

March 1970. Peter Bregg

JUSTIN: He had a lot of fur stuff. We grew up around fur.

PETER BREGG: He's a very sensitive man. If you give him a gift, he accepts it with the sentiment with which it's given. You give me a gift, I should appreciate it. Somebody up in the Arctic gave him this hat, he put it on.

48

On a tour to Rankin Inlet.
Nunavut, August 1970. Peter Bregg

ALEXANDRE: There are so many of these photos. I guess that's why he was good to photographers, that he'd get right into it.

JUSTIN: It was him.

ALEXANDRE: He loved the many peoples of Canada. And he loved going up there and being a part of their world since they were a part of ours.

PETER BREGG: He was, as a photographer's subject, I think the best in the first six years of his term(s)— primarily because he was still very youthful. I think the office hadn't worn him down yet. His problems in his marriage hadn't taken place yet. So up until then, he was very easy, very outgoing, a performer.

Trudeau during a break on a boat trip on the Nahanni River.
Nunavut, August 1970. Peter Bregg

JUSTIN: We can both do that (*Justin wants to demonstrate; Alexandre doesn't*). He's supporting his abs on his elbows … it's just a balance trick, basically. He probably just would have been bored there. It didn't look like there was a lot to do. He's just goofing around. He had lots of little physical tricks that we used to do.

ALEXANDRE: You're never just who you are, when you're in the public view. You create a persona.

PETER BREGG: The discussion went to: "Well, how fit are you?" (Trudeau's reply was) "Well, just watch me." That's the prime minister of Canada, at 50 years of age.

At the Grey Cup game.
Toronto, November 1970. Peter Bregg

ALEXANDRE: I find it's over the top.

JUSTIN: It's over the top. Even for him. It's over the top.

PETER BREGG: *(recalling Trudeau's aides were trying to keep the cape away from him—he had taken it off to do the kickoff.)* CP had a darkroom in the basement (at the stadium). At half-time I'm going back to the darkroom to process my film and Trudeau's coming down the stairs.... I think I'm at the end of the roll of film ... so to finish it off, I just took this frame.... hand the film into the darkroom, get back up to the field, shoot the rest of the game.... The next day ... everybody's used my picture.

In Umraha.

India, January 1971. Peter Bregg

ALEXANDRE: There was this venerable old Iraqi guy who had this tiny little restaurant (in Montreal) that went under for a year. But (Trudeau) kept returning there because he just loved the guy's humanity, his face … and the food wasn't good. But he just really liked this guy … and this kind of reminds me of that.

PETER BREGG: He loved soaking in the local culture whenever he went anywhere. He wanted to know about it, why, and he wanted to be part of it. And doing this bow … it was a sign of respect. And the lower you bow, the more respectful you are. And to see this old lady, bowing as much as she could. And he just matched her, inch for inch, in that bow.

On a pedicab in Jakarta.
Indonesia, January 1971. Peter Bregg

ALEXANDRE: He really liked to reach out to … oldest, poorest, furthest.… He really liked
             communicating at the very basic with …

JUSTIN: … with reality. With the reality of life. He was very, very aware of the magnitude of
             the world, but also of the details. The fact that you make a decision, it touches people
             in the smallest villages. Whether you're going to send aid to this country or that.

ALEXANDRE: It's more … he would really light up when he could communicate or just exchange
             glances with some people from far, from the real edge, in terms of poverty and aging.

Trudeau reflected in the glasses of a woman in Jakarta.
Indonesia, January 1971. Peter Bregg

ALEXANDRE: That's a great photo. Dad or not … it's just a good photo.

PETER BREGG: I was just so taken by this ancient face … with these 20th-century mirrored aviators.
I just ignored Trudeau and I stood near this person with a telephoto lens poised on
this face.… I just kept moving sideways, keeping Trudeau focused in the lens.

On a horse named Sparky at the Calgary Stampede.

July 1971. Ken Pole

CHUCK

MITCHELL: (*reflecting that Trudeau's antics never made him look ridiculous, as other politicians might.*)
His personality allowed him to get away with it.

ALEXANDRE: That's actually a jacket at the McCord Museum now. A collection of Canadian clothes.... He liked the woods and he liked the culture of the woods.

JUSTIN: It was a part of our ancestral history.

PETER BREGG: I think they'd been married just a few months here.... The two of them were lovebirds. They were kissing and hugging.

JUSTIN: I still wear that kilt from time to time. It's the Elliott kilt (Trudeau's mother's family).

Trudeau in Grand Bank.
Newfoundland, August 1971. Peter Bregg

PETER BREGG: You will never, ever see the Canadian prime minister in a photograph with this many people where you don't have a TV camera, reporter, security guard, aide, other photographer. It's just him and those people, the adoration of the people. It's a small town … and I'm sure everybody in town was here that day.

Trudeau and Margaret on a street in St-Pierre,
capital of St-Pierre and Miquelon.
August 1971. Peter Bregg

ALEXANDRE: Look at the styles. They look like some gypsies and sailors.

JUSTIN: They look like some gypsies and sailors in a French port. They were dressing for it. And they were loving it.

PETER BREGG: The guy just had such style. In blue jeans and his Corsican T-shirt and his little scarf.

Trudeau and Margaret on a boat at Lunenberg.
Nova Scotia, August 1971. Peter Bregg

Trudeau and Margaret at a Christmas party
for Liberal workers.
December 1971. Peter Bregg

Trudeau and Jean Chrétien at a press conference.
Ottawa, July 1972. Peter Bregg

ALEXANDRE: Wow, look at the sideburns here!

JUSTIN: They made a good team. They really did.

ALEXANDRE: They enjoyed working together. My father really respected the fact that Chrétien was a doer. That he would roll his sleeves up and get dirty.

Trudeau passes President Nixon the Great Lakes
Water Quality Agreement.
Ottawa, April 1972. CP

ALEXANDRE: Dad always said that Nixon was …

JUSTIN: … a very intelligent, intelligent man.

ALEXANDRE: What were his words? Dark. He had a lot of dark spaces in him. But he was a very, very able, intelligent politician.

JUSTIN: (*referring to tapes Nixon made where he called Trudeau an asshole*)
I remember Dad telling me that Nixon wrote him a nice letter when the tapes came out and said: "Look, when you're in your office and you don't think about what you're saying, you say certain things that aren't meant for public consumption." And Dad mentioned that he really appreciated getting a letter from Nixon.

ALEXANDRE: Nixon was a complex character. And I think my father—I mean, he didn't have great affection for him, but he didn't condemn him outright. He had qualities, Nixon. They didn't really get along.

Trudeau on the campaign plane.

1972. Peter Bregg

THIS PHOTO WAS NOT RELEASED UNTIL AFTER TRUDEAU'S DEATH

JUSTIN: That press plane. Man, that was so much fun. We loved travelling on that plane.

ALEXANDRE: The press plane usually was smoky, boozy … and a lot of people. Too many reporters, not enough story.… There was camaraderie there. It was fun.

PETER BREGG: Anything on the plane was off the record. There was honour among thieves back then and everyone adhered to that rule. Just out of the blue, he looks at me and does this.

On a campaign tour through Stoney Creek.
Ontario, October 1972. Peter Bregg

PETER BREGG: I have pictures where he's staring into the crowd and the TV lights are on his face, and he's got those blue eyes and that smile. And the charisma is just oozing from his pores.

Trudeau tears a protester's placard in half.
Chicoutimi, Quebec, October 1972. Peter Bregg

Trudeau and Margaret with the rock band The Renaissance.
Ottawa, April 1973. Peter Bregg

ALEXANDRE: I don't think he had any … drumming skill. I don't think he could play any instruments.

JUSTIN: I remember him sort of helping us out when we were taking piano lessons.… Remember in church, he always sang with a very deep, deep voice. And he used to sing paddling songs as well … yeah, he would have been just goofing around on the drums there.

JUSTIN: My father was searching for my mother his entire life. And he found her. And he loved her with everything he had and everything that he could. And she loved him absolutely right back. To an extent that I think that both of them didn't quite understand. Because he hadn't allowed himself to go that far over the course of his life, not really. And she hadn't lived enough. She was so young. So that picture, you can really see just the absolute perfection of the fairy tale in that moment of where they were. And that is the energy, right there in that picture, that illustrates what he was to us as a father. I mean, that amount of love and that amount of devotion to our mother and to the idea of the family and to these beings that he created with her.

PETER BREGG: That's another one of my favourites. It's such a tender moment between two people … nose to nose, touching like that.

With Chinese Premier Zhou Enlai
at the Great Hall in Beijing.
October 1973. Peter Bregg

JUSTIN: He always had a real love for China.

ALEXANDRE: He had a real, almost, 'do-not-judge-this-place, it's-much-bigger-than-us attitude'.
              Do not be so quick to know what's going on here—even telling himself that.

In Guyana.
1974. Fred Chartrand

ALEXANDRE: He's playing around.

JUSTIN: No, he's running up, about to jump. He's just warming up to jump over some rocks … or maybe he's faking it. Either way, this was the kind of thing that we grew up with. That could be a picture of Sach (Alexandre) doing that now. That could be a picture of me doing that now. It's just the way we were. The fact that he's doing it and he happens to be prime minister are two things that make the photo interesting. But that's just a guy jumping off rocks in the water.

FRED
CHARTRAND: (*recalling Trudeau had left another pool where the media were and he followed him*)
He knew he was being photographed, so he helped me set it up.

Trudeau and Margaret during a break in the election campaign.
Penticton, British Columbia, June 1974. Russ Mant

JUSTIN: (*commenting on whether his father swam to relax*)
               No! Exercise.

ALEXANDRE: He swam every day.

JUSTIN: Every day. Every evening.

ALEXANDRE: He swam in the morning here (in Montreal). But when he was in politics he used to
               swim every day in the evening.

Trudeau and Margaret.
Ottawa, July 1974. Fred Chartrand

ALEXANDRE: Look how young Mom is.

Margaret and Alexandre greet Trudeau and Justin
after they return from an Arctic vacation.
Ottawa, 1975. Chuck Mitchell

PETER BREGG: *(on the limited occasions they were given to shoot Trudeau with his children)*
Only when they showed up at the airport to say "Hi, Dad" when he came home. Or later on, when he started taking them with him on trips.

Cuban President Fidel Castro with Michel and Margaret.
Havana, January 1976. Fred Chartrand

ALEXANDRE: (Mom) felt very comfortable with Castro…. They had a great time.

JUSTIN: You think of the Caribbean, you think of Latin America being very sort of family-oriented.

ALEXANDRE: They went there feeling very relaxed. They dressed down, knowing that they were going to a poor country that was more values-oriented than material-oriented.

JUSTIN: It made sense to bring Mich along.

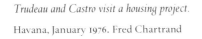

Trudeau and Castro visit a housing project.
Havana, January 1976. Fred Chartrand

ALEXANDRE: He really respected Castro.... Castro's just about as smart a man as you can find. And I think not all world politicians or heads of state were necessarily ...

JUSTIN: Smart men.

ALEXANDRE: ... or intellectuals, you know? Castro, you could talk to Castro about anything. He's an expert on anything and everything. He's a genius, really. So I think beyond politics, my father just really liked exchanging ideas with the man. Because he was so intelligent and (had) such a deep view of the world and of the ideas in it.

Margaret and Trudeau swing Alexandre in
a goodbye gesture before flying to Japan,.
Vancouver airport, October 1976. Doug Ball

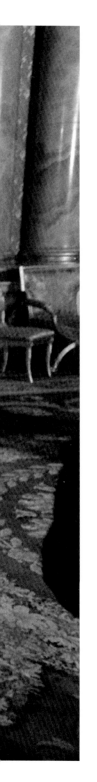

At the end of a photo op with the Queen and
Group of Seven leaders, Buckingham Palace.
London, May 1977. Doug Ball

ALEXANDRE: He was in the room—he told us this story because we asked him about the pirouette—
and he said there was kind of a little bit of a shuffle on the part of the statesmen to get
next to the Queen for the photo op. And perhaps because he was on the far side of the
table or perhaps because the whole thing kind of came off as kind of …

JUSTIN: … hokey.

ALEXANDRE: Hokey … you know, not very graceful. Or perhaps because he had no chance … he was
not going to get (the prime spot in) the photo op so he might as well … so he let them
leave and they were kind of rushing and stumbling forward…. It naturally came to him (as)
just an expression of autonomy, of independence. And some photographer … was lucky.

JUSTIN: It wasn't meant to be a picture.

ALEXANDRE: It wasn't disrespectful.

JUSTIN: It was playful.

ALEXANDRE: It was playful and it was sort of making fun of …

JUSTIN: … the whole pomp. And not the Queen herself…. He's just defusing a bit the situation,
as much for himself as for anybody else.

DOUG BALL: I'd already done the straight-on family picture. So I moved over to get Trudeau in the
foreground, which might be better for Canadian papers, and they start moving away and
he did the pirouette. I just fired it—from my chest or something. Looked up, saw the
pirouette and bang! Pure horseshit luck. It really was.

Alexandre, Trudeau and Michel.
Ottawa, 1979. The Canadian Press

JUSTIN: It was something that we took for granted, but he came home just about every single night to spend a little bit of time with us. And he'd then work.... It was an absolute rule: The PM went home at a particular time.

Michel, Alexandre and Justin in the prime minister's office.
Ottawa, March 1979. Peter Bregg

ALEXANDRE: (*recalling an official trip to Mongolia with their father*)
We got in a heavy fight. And one of us, I think Mich, was in tears. There was a scene. And this was with the president there. And (Dad) says: "Well, kids, I think you've insulted them. And I think an apology is in order, for your behaviour."

JUSTIN: That's right.

ALEXANDRE: Because you were the oldest, I'm like: "I'm not apologizing." There was this big, Jabba the Hut kind of….

JUSTIN: Very strongly Genghis, Mongolian, impressive man. Stoic.

ALEXANDRE: And I remember, you were almost in tears with the thought of having to do it. He (Dad) brought him up. "He has something to say."

JUSTIN: "My son has something to say to you." And I just say: "I'm sorry for having—what was it? —ruined your evening."

ALEXANDRE: We were such a disturbance at the (banquet) … in Asia, kids are very discreet. We were little barbarians.

JUSTIN: We really were.

ALEXANDRE: Little barbarians … we had fun.

JUSTIN: Yeah.

Trudeau with Alexandre (jumping) and Michel
at 24 Sussex Drive.
Ottawa, May 1979. Peter Bregg

JUSTIN: We had two things with Dad, in terms of jumping off high heights. There was 'Fly Like a Birdie' and there was 'Break Your Fall'. I think Sacha is showing a good bridge between 'Fly Like A Birdie' and 'Break Your Fall'. As we got older, he used to help us land . . . so we could jump from incredible heights. I think the highest we ever did was about 15 feet off of a ranger tower in . . .

ALEXANDRE: Manitoba. He liked to get us to jump off things. I think he thought it was important that we be physically . . . not fearless, but physically . . .

JUSTIN AND
ALEXANDRE: Confident.

ALEXANDRE: Rational, physical—it was very important. Not that it was a duty. It's a rational physicality.

JUSTIN: It's knowing what your limits are and playing within them. But, at the same time, making sure those limits are pushed to the edge of what it is you can do.

ALEXANDRE: Making sure you know your limits and you're confident within those limits.

PETER BREGG: *(recalling this was the only time he was asked to go to 24 Sussex for a photo session with the boys)* We showed up, not knowing what for. And we spent about half an hour watching him at play with the kids. When he was with them, they were fearless. . . . They would just jump. They knew he was there.

JUSTIN: One of the things that he was aware of, becoming a father when he was 50, was this idea … the classic story of someone who has kids too late won't be able to toss around the ball in the backyard. Well, he went out of his way to demonstrate to everyone and to himself and to us mostly (that wasn't true).

ALEXANDRE: But that was him. It was not just about parenting.

JUSTIN: Now that ultimate Frisbee is such a big thing, I have friends of mine sending me that picture periodically (saying), "Hey, your dad used to play?" I'm like, yeah, I've seen it.

Trudeau at the Quebec Liberal convention.
Montreal, October 1979. Doug Ball

ALEXANDRE: He loved women. He loved women.

JUSTIN: He liked the person he was, the side of him that they brought out, that they liked. He spent so much time in his time being focused on intellectual pursuits and everything like that …

ALEXANDRE: Be careful!

JUSTIN: But so focused on the typically 'man's world' sort of things that when he could—especially in those times—when he could show that he was more relaxed.

ALEXANDRE: We're being too serious about this photo.

JUSTIN: He's got a good little hip action going there.

Justin, Michel and Alexandre at their father's swearing-in.
Ottawa, March 1980. Ron Poling

ALEXANDRE: We're lucky we're on our chairs, we're not fighting. We were …

JUSTIN: … scrappy youngsters.

ALEXANDRE: Scrappy. Because of his getting us to jump everywhere, we were kind of hyper kids.

JUSTIN: Very physical.

RON POLING: It was a long ceremony and I was fascinated by how the three boys managed to sit
                 through it. Their colourful boots and their expressions made it a priceless moment.

Trudeau and his sons beginning a drive to the prime
minister's cottage at Harrington Lake, Que.
Ottawa, September 1980. Fred Chartrand

JUSTIN: We would go up to the country place (Harrington Lake) on weekends and we'd take
            the car and we'd be followed by the security guys. And it was Dad driving, obviously.
            Me sitting in the passenger's seat with Mich sitting right in front of me and Sach sitting in
            the middle sort of hump, straddling the gear shift. And we all fit in perfectly great.

ALEXANDRE: We were just little kids … it was fun.

JUSTIN: Oh, it was fun. It was great. It wasn't a long drive but it was a time where we got to be
            absolutely alone with Dad. And in something that was actually ours. 'Cause the car
            belonged to us—or to him—whereas the government cars, the limos, the house, even
            the country house we were going to was all property of the government. So the car
            always represented a sense of 'Well, this is not…. This can't be taken away if we lose an
            election sort of thing.'

ALEXANDRE: (Trudeau and Lévesque had) known each other a long time … but they didn't really get along, even back then. They just had different styles. But by this time they were …

JUSTIN: … fairly locked into understanding that their individual views of Canada were mutually irreconcilable.

ALEXANDRE: They were pitted against each other.

Trudeau and Alexandre tour tombs at Madain Saleh.

Saudi Arabia, November 1980. Andy Clark

ALEXANDRE: It was a freaky place for a six-year-old kid.... These (trips) were overwhelming. I'm looking
               at my expression . . .

JUSTIN: A little scared. You're hanging on to Dad very tight there.

ALEXANDRE: I was awfully young to be in that context.

JUSTIN: It was wonderful.

Saudi Arabian Oil Minister Sheik Yamani and Trudeau
dance in desert while Alexandre watches.
Saudi Arabia, November 1980. Fred Chartrand

ALEXANDRE: It was just amazing … all these tents. It was in Ramadan … waiting till dark to eat. And at night they were cutting goats. I was walking around and goats were being slaughtered by the dozen. And the camels were coming in and it was just magical.… There they were doing the desert dance. I was seven. It was an amazing experience.… You don't forget this experience.… It was not a photo op.… It was like two tribes meeting in the desert. And there he is dancing. He brought his own jallabiya there, which was a beautiful blue silk. They wear the white silk, which I had on. What a moment.

FRED
CHARTRAND: I got my shot but I had no way of getting it back to Canada. The next day we went to Yemen, where it took three hours to transmit the photo over lousy telephone lines. The picture ran everywhere and John Crosbie, the Conservative finance critic, mocked Trudeau for dancing 'sheik to sheik' while Canada's economy was in a mess.

Trudeau and Alexandre at the pyramids near Cairo.

Egypt 1980. Andy Clark

ALEXANDRE: For some reason—I don't think it was mine—I had to ride a camel. But the camels came in off the desert at like four in the morning. Therefore, I was woken up at five in the morning to get on the camel that had just come in off the desert and it was in a bad mood.

He didn't enjoy the ride. Later, at the pyramids, his father suggested he ride another one.

I'm like: "I'm not getting on unless you're getting on with me."

Trudeau on the Rio Negro, a tributary of the Amazon.
Brazil, January 1981. Andy Clark

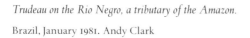

ALEXANDRE: He was the kind of man, you put him in a canoe, anywhere … it was a skill that he had.

JUSTIN: He loved to canoe.

JUSTIN: We never saw that face. That's … 'What do you want me to do here? What do you expect of me?' But he would never say that to us because, you know, he knew exactly what we expected of him and he lived up to it.

PETER BREGG: (*recalling that before this shot Trudeau had held his nose to show what the British Parliament would have to do when they passed the Canadian constitutional act*)
He did the motion. And we all missed it. So I sat down in front and I put the camera up and I kept it there for the whole news conference. And just then he said, "Well, you know … " Bingo!

Justin, Michel and Alexandre greet Trudeau

after a trip to Europe.

Ottawa, April 1981. Andy Clark

Trudeau at Remembrance Day ceremonies
with Justin, Michel and Alexandre.
Ottawa, November 1981. Fred Chartrand

Trudeau in Commons after reaching an accord with the premiers of all the provinces except Quebec for the patriation of the Constitution. Ottawa, November 1981. Andy Clark

ALEXANDRE: It was a national achievement, but a strategic achievement since it was something that many people had tried (to do) and failed before.... He didn't have any vision of Canada depending on, stemming from, anything else. He thought we had our mechanism for guidance, our own tiller.... He had no disrespect for history of any kind. In fact, knowing who we are now means that we can....

JUSTIN: ... build on it.

ALEXANDRE: He was a jurist by trade. (He thought the fact) that our essential legal document was not in our hands was a travesty.

Trudeau watches Queen Elizabeth sign the Constitution proclamation.

Ottawa, April 1982. Ron Poling

ALEXANDRE: He was not a writer or a poet in an artistic sense, but he really felt that this, the document, the Constitution, was sort of something that could express in a deep way, almost a poetry of who we are. So he's jubilant here, in this picture…. He didn't spend a lot of time thinking about the British Crown and he was totally against titles. But in the context of the Constitution here is the monarch of our country empowering us to take possession of our essential document. It meant a lot to him.

RON POLING: There was a sea of people on the lawn of Parliament Hill. Even from our vantage point, on the tall media riser, it was hard to see the Queen and prime minister. Through our lenses, however, we could see their faces and we knew we were witnessing a special moment.

Trudeau at Uplands Airport, after the Queen departs
following the proclamation of the Constitution.
Ottawa, April 1982. Andy Clark

ALEXANDRE: (The pirouette) became a signature piece. As many things did. He just did it spontaneously.
              I mean, he just wore flowers for the effect and they slowly were molded into trademarks.

JUSTIN: It got a great reaction.

ALEXANDRE: Punctuation. For an important moment.

Trudeau and Queen Elizabeth.

B.C. Place Stadium, Vancouver, March 1983. Peter Bregg

ALEXANDRE: The fact is, if you sit there for three hours with a camera, and watch someone, you can get that person picking their nose, you can get them yawning.

JUSTIN: You can get them looking really angrily at the Queen, it looks like. But he's actually deep in thought and looking over towards the clock tower over that way.

ALEXANDRE: Or there's a drip coming off the ceiling.... I think he got along with the Queen. I don't think she was terribly fond of his public irreverence towards her... but I gather that she always thought him an enjoyable prime minister. He respected her. He thought she was a very savvy, wise woman. And someone you could work with.

PETER BREGG: When you take a picture, quite often it's just by accident. You don't see it until you get in the darkroom. And every once in a while, you see it when you make it. And you get a real buzz.... I knew I had a picture. And because of the perceived idea I had of their relationship, it told me the same story.

Trudeau with Michel in Ohrid.
Yugoslavia, June 1982. Bill Grimshaw

JUSTIN: It was a huge part of us, growing up…. He used to take one of us on each big trip.

ALEXANDRE: It was a time when we got to spend time with Dad too. Alone.

JUSTIN: That's the thing.

Trudeau with guitarist Liona Boyd at the ACTRA awards.
Toronto, April 1983. Tim Clark

TIM CLARK: Typically photographers are wisked into the room for a brief photo op with the PM.
The modern political leader points and laughs gregariously when the cameras are in place
for these brief sessions. But there was no showmanship here. They just appeared to be two
people having a good time.

Trudeau escorts actress Margot Kidder to a dinner
in his honour at the Canadian Embassy.
Washington, April 1983. Peter Bregg

ALEXANDRE: He liked women. And a lot of them liked him, which he was happy about.

Trudeau with Diana, Princess of Wales.
Ottawa, June 1983. Andy Clark

JUSTIN: It was like a family picnic thing.

ALEXANDRE: Again, it's the fact that not too many prime ministers had young families at the time and therefore weren't doing that thing anymore.

JUSTIN: He really didn't thrust us out there.

ALEXANDRE: He had to make an effort. It's not easy for him, going out there. Just by going out there, he would have to talk and shake a thousand hands. But he used to say: "I have to accept that." He used to say to my Mom--that was a problem --"We have to accept this existence." And we were in it too. We didn't know anything else so it was fine with us. But it must have been exhausting. And yet, it was very important to him to be able to live normally, at the same time.

Michel, Justin and Alexandre with Trudeau
at the Parthenon.
Athens, August 1983. Peter Bregg

PETER BREGG: (*on Trudeau taking his children on official trips*)
They would take turns. It's rare that all three would go.

Alexandre skis with his father and a security guard.
Davos, Switzerland, January 1984. Andy Clark

ALEXANDRE: He knew his limits. Perfectly. He knew his physical presence from start to finish. He knew how to calculate what he could and couldn't do and he didn't make mistakes very often. Ever. He didn't fall very often skiing.

Truduea, with Justin, Alexandre and Michel, says farewell
at the Liberal convention that chose John Turner as leader.
Ottawa, June 1984. The Canadian Press

ALEXANDRE: I was just a little kid, but I found that a very emotional time.

JUSTIN: Extremely emotional. Extremely educational as well (watching the recap that night of Trudeau's political career.) I think that was the first time I saw 'Just watch me,' the first time I realized there had been a referendum in 1980.

ALEXANDRE: It was amazing how outside of the loop we were when he was in politics. It was just not about politics.

JUSTIN: It wasn't. It was about growing up.

At the Liberal leadership convention to elect a new leader.
Ottawa, June 1984. Chuck Mitchell

PETER BREGG: *(recalling how his fellow photographer, the very tall Chuck Mitchell, hoisted a monopod with a remote on it from the pool position by the stage so they could both get Trudeau and the crowd)*
The thing is, the next day when (John) Turner won (the leadership), we did the same thing.... Two days in a row, we scored high with Chuck and the stick.

At the Liberal leadership convention.
Ottawa, June 1984. Chuck Mitchell

JUSTIN: Everyone says that's a perfect example of the gunslinger pose. That's him doing the gunslinger pose for them. Giving them what they wanted. And pleased about it. And you can see in his eyes, recognizing the appreciation and very happy.

Trudeau leaves 24 Sussex Drive, after resigning as prime minister.
Ottawa, June 1984. Andrew Vaughan

ALEXANDRE: He was overjoyed to be getting out.

CHUCK

MITCHELL: In some regards, we (photographers) hated to lose him. In other regards, we were quite happy, you know, to have a break from him.

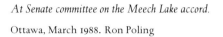

At Senate committee on the Meech Lake accord.
Ottawa, March 1988. Ron Poling

A L E X A N D R E :   There was a sense there, and this is not aimed at anyone, but sometimes he would lament. You know? When he had to fight Meech and all this. He says: I don't want to be fighting this stuff. I just do it because no one else is.

Trudeau waits to vote on the Charlottetwon
accord on constitutional changes.
Montreal, October 1992. Tom Hanson

ALEXANDRE: *(explaining his father's views on the Charlottetown accord)*
It was deal-making. And he didn't think we should play around with the Constitution
that way. You don't deal-make with the Constitution.

Trudeau votes in advance poll in federal election.
Montreal, October 1993. Ryan Remiorz

RYAN
REMIORZ: For elections and referendums, what we'd usually do is call his office and they'd say: "Mr. Trudeau will be voting in the advance poll" or whatever. And if they don't, you just have to gamble. They used to put the voters lists up on the telephone polls. You could just check to see what polling station he'd be at. And you'd just sit there and wait.... He usually voted in the morning anyway.... He loved the camera. There was no denying it. In (retirement) he wouldn't really pose. But he usually knew that cameras would be there so it's no coincidence that more often then not he showed up in one of his classic outfits.

At a news conference announcing the release of his book, Memoirs.
Montreal, November 1993. Ryan Remiorz

RYAN
REMIORZ: It's one of his many classic poses that he used to strike. There was no real magic or secret to it. It was a nice moment and I got it. When he died, I was in Sydney (covering the 2000 Olympics). And somebody sent me an email of all the front pages the next day. And so many of the papers used that picture, which to be quite honest I'd forgotten all about. It was very flattering.

Trudeau and Margaret at Michel's memorial service.
Montreal, November 1998. Ryan Remiorz

Ryan

Remiorz: He just looked so pale and sallow. And obviously, I think that would happen to anyone regardless of their age, if they lose a child. We're so used to seeing him as a vibrant outdoorsman. And then that day he just looked very, very old.... It was just such a different image of a person that I'd taken pictures of for almost 20 years.

Trudeau, Alexandre, Margaret and Justin leaving
Michel's memorial service.
Montreal, November 1998. Ryan Remiorz

ALEXANDRE: It's a haunting photo. What can you say?

JUSTIN: (*explaining the handkerchief he is holding had belonged to Michel*)
That's him. That little spot of red is him in that picture.

RYAN
REMIORZ: It was quite an emotional moment, I have to admit. If I wasn't shooting, I think it would
have been quite easy to get overwhelmed. When they all came out, it was kind of interesting
that he … looked over at us at one point. That's when I got him. And just the look in his
eye was one of, I think, a combination of hate and understanding. They made no attempt
to keep us away from there and he knew it was part of Canadian history and he just showed
the strength he always has in supporting his family. And I think it must have been extremely
difficult for him to walk out of there and not break down.… I think a big part of him died
when his son died. And there was no hiding that, regardless of whether he cried or not.
I think you can just see it, the way he's looking at us. He looks very empty.

Trudeau walks to his law office.
Montreal, October 1999. Ryan Remiorz

JUSTIN: When I turned 25 I sat down with him in his office and I said: 'Dad, you're healthy …' But I'd actually had a friend of mine, an older friend of mine, who'd just had a talk with his father about this sort of stuff and he said: 'Justin, have you had a talk with your dad about that?' … So I sat down with Dad and it was a half hour, 45-minute conversation in his office in which I spent the entire time in tears just trying to articulate all these questions. Where do you want to be buried? Are you going to want a state funeral? And he gave me a number of different answers on that. He said: 'Well, you know, I'm pretty sure they'll want to do something. So whatever they'll want to do is going to be fine. But definitely (I) want to be with my dad and mum in St-Rémi.' And he was so wonderful during that conversation with me. And that, in a certain sense, sustained me through the days of pulling it together.

ALEXANDRE: He was an old man for about two, three years. And then he died. And here, he's an old man.

RYAN
REMIORZ: He was very accessible. He'd walk to work every day…. Everybody would take a look. They'd stop and chat and he was very approachable. (On this day) he said: 'What are you here for today?' And I said: 'Well, it's your 80TH birthday, I was wondering if I could get some pictures.' And he said: 'Snap away.'

RCMP pallbearers carry Trudeau's coffin under the arches
of the Peace Tower.
Ottawa, October 2000. Jonathan Hayward

JUSTIN: *(about the ride into Ottawa with his father's hearse)*
There was a man on the side of Colonel By Drive, as we were just coming along the canal. And, you know, it wasn't publicized that this was the route we were going on but it was pretty obvious, you know? The hearse, the Mounties, everything.... No one knew what magnitude it would have in terms of (public) reaction. And this one guy just sort of stood there and just quietly (did a pirouette). That just hit me so much that someone would ... be so touched by it. The thing is, he (Trudeau) never did a pirouette for us. That wasn't him. But it was a symbol of him, the person, and the energy that was behind sort of all the pomp.

ALEXANDRE: ... that he (Trudeau) had touched someone.

JUSTIN: It was overwhelming.

Alexandre and Justin watch as their father's coffin
is loaded into a hearse.
Ottawa, 2000. Andrew Vaughan

ALEXANDRE: (*on bringing their father's body to Ottawa to lie in state*)
I was a little bit worried. I was like: 'What are we bringing him to Ottawa for? What are we doing this for?' Then I went and escaped to the country, to the lake, and I was just there and I was just really worried. How could we bring him to Ottawa and just leave him there?

JUSTIN: But he was well taken care of. There's no question about it.... When they installed his casket in the Hall of Honour, in the Parliament Buildings, they gave us a half an hour just no cameras, no nothing, right before the PM showed up and the Governor General. We got a little time with him there. But that was still sort of ceremonial. It wasn't fully private. But it was ... for me, that was really sort of seeing him—well, sorry, not seeing him, but seeing the casket and seeing it within the Parliament Buildings, really sort of centred it right for me in a very strong way.

ALEXANDRE: (*sounding surprised*)
                       That was fun.

JUSTIN: The train was fun.

ALEXANDRE: We were kind of dazed through the whole thing. And sort of spontaneously people would be there and someone said: "Maybe you guys should go acknowledge that they were there."

JUSTIN: Absolutely. And we got them to slow down the train.

ALEXANDRE: (And) acknowledge that they were there. And so we would stay out. And it became something joyous, you know.... I was just thankful.

JUSTIN: People kept saying: "Oh, it's so nice that you're coming to show yourself." I'm like: "What? Are you kidding? You're not watching us. We're watching you." That's what they didn't get. We got to watch them. We had the best seats in the world to watch everyone celebrate our father.

ALEXANDRE: It was surprising to me. I remember I was truly touched by how much people liked him. Because I liked him a lot.

Trudeau's funeral.

Notre Dame Basilica, October 2000. Paul Chiasson

ALEXANDRE: It was a surprising event.

JUSTIN: He braced us for it because he had lost his father at 15. He'd always sort of say: When I'm gone, you're going to have to do this and that. And he wouldn't really dwell on it, but he'd be aware of that. And in the sense, I think we knew that, especially in later years, when he was retired and pulled back from the public life, that there would be something big happening (when he died) that we'd sort of deal with.

ALEXANDRE: What was crazy about this and a little bit overwhelming was the magnitude of the event.

PAUL
CHIASSON: (*only news photographer allowed inside the cathedral*)
Rarely (except for the funeral) have I felt that I was covering a real, major Canadian event. It was unreal. It doesn't get any bigger than that, I don't think.